The Gangs of Chinatown: The History and Legacy of Chinese Street Gangs in America

By Charles River Editors

A picture of Chinatown in Los Angeles

About Charles River Editors

Charles River Editors is a boutique digital publishing company, specializing in bringing history back to life with educational and engaging books on a wide range of topics. Keep up to date with our new and free offerings with this 5 second sign up on our weekly mailing list, and visit Our Kindle Author Page to see other recently published Kindle titles.

We make these books for you and always want to know our readers' opinions, so we encourage you to leave reviews and look forward to publishing new and exciting titles each week.

Introduction

A picture of Chinatown in New York City

San Francisco Chinatown, September 4, 1977, 2:00 a.m. Despite it being the middle of the night, Chinatown was still a hive of activity. Fresh produce glistening with dew was being delivered by vegetable vendors at grocery stores. Chinese barbeque chefs at neighborhood restaurants were preparing juicy roast duck and sticky sweet red barbeque pork for both the late-night crowd and tomorrow's lunch rush. Walking down the dense streets, vibrant Cantonese could be heard from Chinatown residents, some jockeying for a seat at late-night dim sum restaurants, a favorite Cantonese staple of little steamed and fried dumplings and pastries.

The restaurant Golden Dragon was no different, except on this night, instead of a peaceful late-night meal, a barrage of bullets would spray into the restaurant, unleashed by gunmen from the notorious Chinese Joe Boys street gang. The gangsters were aiming for their archrivals, the Wah Ching and the Hop Sing Boys. The attack was a revenge strike, as a Joe Boys street soldier had been killed in a running gun battle after a Wah Ching gang ambush on the Fourth of July at the Ping Yuen housing project in Chinatown. The Joe Boys were furious for revenge, and two months later, the death of their fellow gangster still fresh in their minds, the Joe Boys struck. An opportunity presented itself when a lookout spotted Wah Ching and Hop Sing gangsters at the Golden Dragon Restaurant.

Ultimately, the gang shooting failed to kill a single street gang member. Instead, five innocent people were killed along with another 11 wounded. Chinatown and the city were shocked. Chinese gangs, once only a subject spoken in hushed tones among the residents of Chinatown, was now front-page news in America. Although the shooting was a shock to mainstream America, the attack represented a culmination of years of gang violence in the Chinese community. For years, gangs had killed dozens of people in Chinatown, an area that was both a tourist attraction and home to thousands of poor, mostly Chinese-born, immigrants. Most casualties in the gang wars of Chinatown had been criminals, combatants in vicious street combat. But the Golden Dragon shooting was different. This time the battle occurred in a popular restaurant, with victims being innocent civilians with no connection or knowledge to gangs or the revenge origins of the shooting. Chinatown would be changed forever after the Golden Dragon Massacre.

Chinese gangs have been a part of the fabric of American Chinatowns since the first Chinese immigrants arrived in the nineteenth century to work on the railroads. Faced with intense racism and systematic oppression from mainstream society, secret societies called tongs were organized in the urban Chinatowns. These societies provided much needed social and financial support for the Chinese migrants who were treated as pariahs by American society. Eventually, as Chinese immigration increased after the passage of the 1965 Immigration Act, Chinese gangs evolved too. Chinese street gangs, ranging from the Ghost Shadows of urban New York Chinatown to the middle-class Taiwanese Americans that filled the gangs of Southern California, underground Chinese crime groups have continued to evolve and change in America.

The Gangs of Chinatown: The History and Legacy of Chinese Street Gangs in America looks at how some of the gangs formed, what their activities were like, and their impact. Along with pictures depicting important people, places, and events, you will learn about the gangs of Chinatown like never before.

Background

The Tiandihui began in seventeenth century China as a religious and political secret society dedicated to the overthrow of the ruling Qing dynasty and the restoration of the Ming dynasty. Rites emphasized brotherhood and solidarity and members were expected to regard each other as blood brothers. Individual local chapters had a clearly defined hierarchy and structure reinforced by secret, solemn ceremonies where members were sworn to silence and obedience.

In the early nineteenth century, the city of Hong Kong, ruled by the British, became a center for the Tiandihui and its members were frequently arrested by British police who tried (unsuccessfully) to suppress the organization. Political turmoil in China led to a number of famines and increasing numbers of Chinese began to emigrate to escape poverty. Initially the majority of these migrants went to other South East Asian countries but during the early to mid-nineteenth century, increasing numbers left for the United States. In America, as in other countries that saw large Chinese communities, the migrants formed tight-knit, self-contained communities where most of the new arrivals did not speak a non-Chinese language and so remained segregated socially and culturally from the new area in which they found themselves living.

In 1848, gold was discovered in California, causing a frenzied boom in the population of the state. However, just five years later the gold had effectively been panned out and California (and most of America) entered a financial depression. The economic situation in the Golden State was grim, but one area that was not affected by this slowdown was the shipping industry. One byproduct of this trans-Pacific trade was an influx of Chinese laborers.

In 1854, 16,000 Chinese arrived in America, four times the number than in previous years. These early waves of Chinese immigrants were generally poor, fleeing the turmoil of the Opium Wars, the Taiping Rebellion and a series of natural disasters that had led to famine and poverty in China. Large numbers of skilled Chinese workers suddenly became available as a low-cost labor force in the Western United States. Within a short time, Chinese workers became a significant part of the labor force in California and many white Americans became resentful of these foreign workers.

To counteract what they saw as a threat to white workers, American organized labor quickly established a movement against the Chinese migrants. The indictment was centered on: "The contract labor system, but the inability or unwillingness of the legislature or the courts to control the abuses of the system, and the continued support of the Chinese by the capitalists in railroads, mining and agriculture, resulted in a generalized attack on the Chinese."[1]

---

[1] Paul Takagi and Tony Platt, *Behind the Gilded Ghetto: An Analysis of Race, Class and Crime in Chinatown* (Crime and Social Justice, no. 9, 1978).

Large numbers of white workers joined an "Anti-Coolie Committee" chaired by D. Supple, who noted, "Did not blame the Chinese for being here but thought the blame belonged to that class of employers and manufacturers who employed them to reduce the wages of white labor."[2]

A small number of people did speak out against this discrimination with some newspapers noting that banning the Chinese from entering the United States was "stupid" and "absurd" and would devastate certain industries, as "a third of our (grain) harvest was gathered by Asiatic labor."[3]

However, when the economic problems led to a lack of employment opportunities, some politicians began to use fear of Chinese migrants to attract votes from white working-class voters. For instance, Henry Haight, elected governor of California in 1867, stated it was necessary for "Germans, Irishmen, and Americans to establish beyond question that California is to be ruled by white men, and not by Chinamen."[4]

When the Central Pacific Railroad was completed in 1869, this massive project did not bring the immediate prosperity it had promised. Widespread unemployment became a state-wide problem, freight rates remained high and thousands of white and Chinese workers found themselves unemployed. The white workers reacted with rage towards the railroad companies and other corporations but their fury was also directed towards Chinese migrants. A series of laws were enacted by the California State Supreme Court specifically directed against Chinese migrants:

> "They held that no Chinese should be permitted to give evidence against any white person; the California legislature rejected the 15th Amendment in denying citizenship for the Chinese; Chinese were excluded from the public schools."

These rulings simply increased widespread public resentment against the Chinese community and this in turn led to Chinese communities becoming more isolated. The editor of the Sonora Flag newspaper, generally sympathetic to the plight of Chinese migrants, wrote that:

> "Whites have unrestricted license to rob and kill the unfortunate Chinamen. Much as we dislike the Chinamen, they should be protected by the government since they pay a heavy tax to it."

In 1882, after a great deal of political pressure was exerted within California, the Chinese Exclusion Act was enacted, effectively barring more Chinese migrants from entering America. As the harsh immigration restrictions against the Chinese came into effect, the number of young Chinese in America was greatly reduced.

----

[2] Takagi and Platt.

[3] Takagi and Platt.

[4] Takagi and Platt.

While a great many young white men became involved in crime due to economic hardships; in general, Chinese youth were considered, and reported by American authorities, to be "law-abiding and hard-working students." In fact, many social scientists openly pondered why the Chinese communities in America had such extremely low youth delinquency rates compared to communities of European ethnic origin.

However, the seemingly peaceful Chinese communities in America were already seeing increasing levels of clandestine triad activity. When they arrived, most Chinese lived in very poor conditions. Chinatowns were generally neglected by the American government, leaving most infrastructure in a very poor state. A description of the conditions of Los Angeles Chinatown in 1916 illustrates the conditions in which many Chinese migrants lived:

> "Kitchens were ... filled with rubbish and decaying matter, swarming with flies, overrun with cockroaches and rats. Vermin swarmed in the slime found in the rotting boards under the insanitary, leaking sinks. ... In the rear of one restaurant there was a large, deep hole near the cellar door, filled with several feet of water and ... a dead chicken and rotting garbage floating in the water polluted the air throughout the neighborhood."

This situation was not unique to Los Angeles and the Chinatown areas in many American cities gained a rather sinister reputation.

> "In addition to fear of disease, those who ventured into Chinatown had also to reckon with the ruffians who frequented its narrow streets."

Of Los Angeles's bordello-ridden Chinatown, a California investigating commission observed that until 1913: "It seemed hardly safe to walk through the streets at night on account of the drunken gangs and other disorderly groups of men."

Even in 1928, a visitor to Chicago's Chinatown still described "cafes, saloons, nightclubs, and ... men and women of suspicious character" and "in the night the street is so dimly lit that it is always safer to walk in bands."

According to a San Francisco police officer, "There was hardly a day that someone was not killed, even white people killed by accident, as shot[s] was [sic] flying everywhere." In 1889, Rudyard Kipling witnessed a shootout between a Mexican player and Chinese dealer in a Chinatown poker parlor in San Francisco. Kipling escaped with his life by hiding under the table. On the basis of this frightening experience, he advised others to "not knock about the Chinese quarter at night and alone." White tourists in New York City's Chinatown also risked murder on the streets, and some were injured when caught in the middle of a shootout.

The lawlessness and poverty of the Chinatowns in many American cities proved to be the ideal environment for the growth of the triads and organized crime.

The Emergence of the Tongs and Chinese Youth Gangs

It is believed that the first Chinese triads were established in America in San Francisco in the 1850s during the initial wave of Chinese immigration. Most Chinese communities, in America as elsewhere, were ruled by either a dominant family or by associations or guilds. These groupings provided all kinds of support and help for migrants and became an important part of Chinese migrant society in America.

However, because they were not members of an appropriate family or did not belong to the right guild, many of the poorest of the Chinese migrants were left out of these organizations. Without support, they began to form their own groups. These groups quickly became known as "tongs" from the Chinese word for a hall or meeting place. In America, the term tong was generally used as a synonym for the word triad. Unlike the existing guilds, which often required members to belong to one family or to come from a particular area or village, tongs were loose affiliations with few membership requirements. Tongs quickly spread across America with groups in most Chinatowns in major American cities.

These tongs provided many valuable social services to their members such as job referrals and help with housing. These organizations were often the only source of these important services for large numbers of Chinese migrants who were unable to join other guilds or associations. The tongs also played an important role within Chinatowns as mediators for both group and individual conflicts and in providing protection for members of the Chinese community.

This was very necessary as antipathy towards Chinese migrants became widespread in America. The California Committee on Mines and Mining Interests in 1856 were fairly typical when they called the Chinese "a disgusting scab upon the fair face of society—a putrefying sore upon the body politic."

This left many Chinese with only their own people to rely on and that generally meant the tongs. ''No matter what you need, you go to the tong," says Ko-lin Chin, a professor at the Rutgers School of Criminal Justice, describing nineteenth century San Francisco. ''If a Chinese man dies and he doesn't want to be buried in the United States, the tongs help ship the body back to China. If you need a notice read in English. If you need a loan." Tongs also provided the Chinese community with prostitution, opium, and gambling dens. According to Chin, many tongs had an associated street gang or a connection to organized crime.

As resentment against Chinese migrants in America increased in the latter part of the nineteenth century, many migrants looked to the tongs for protection from increasing levels of violence directed at Chinese communities.

For example, in May 1887, in an area close to the Snake River in Oregon and known as Hells Canyon, a group of men from nearby Wallowa County rode out to attack a Chinese work camp.

At least thirty Chinese migrants were killed with many of the bodies showing signs of torture. A quantity of gold was also stolen from the camp and the identities of men involved, some as young as fifteen, were known in the local area. In 1888 six men were indicted by a Grand Jury for the murders, but only three were brought to trial and all were found innocent. No one was ever punished for the commission of these murders. With events like this making it all too clear to Chinese migrants that they could not rely on the US justice system to protect them or to punish crimes against Asian migrants, it is unsurprising that so many sought self-protection through the tongs.

The majority of tong activities were entirely legal and carried out within the businesses or jobs of members. These members paid a fee to attend social gatherings such as banquets and picnics where they would meet other members of the tong. The leaders of these tongs came to wield a great deal of influence on the daily lives of group members and became powerful people within Chinatown communities.

However, in addition to their legal roles, many tong leaders developed relationships with youth street gangs, using them as soldiers for criminal operations including opium smuggling, gambling and brothels as well as narcotics and human trafficking. Gradually, tongs came to be regarded by law enforcement organizations as principally organized crime groups, similar to the groups seen in other migrant communities in America. Despite this, tongs remained firmly rooted in the communities from which they sprang and continued to perform many useful social functions in addition to their criminal activities.

In the years following the end of World War Two, the situation within many Chinatowns began to change, with youth gangs emerging, which were completely independent of the tongs. What was referred to as "delinquent youth culture" became an issue across America in the 1950s and 1960s, affecting every ethnic grouping. Many Chinese youth gangs began as innocuous martial arts clubs, basically self-help groups often led by masters who were also tong members. Members of these early gangs spent most of their time practicing martial arts and they also protected their neighborhoods from unruly out-of-towners.

However, by the early 1960s, some of these gangs were beginning to become predatory, attacking businesses, other gangs and even passers-by in Chinatown areas. The earliest known Chinese street gang, the Continentals, was formed in 1961 in San Francisco. Members were mainly high school students who established the gang as a means of self-protection. Over the years, other notable Chinese gangs were created in other US cities. These included the White Eagles, Black Eagles, Ghost Shadows, and the Flying Dragons.

By the early 1970s, young Asian gangsters roamed the streets of many Chinatowns in America, terrorizing neighborhoods, demanding food and money from local merchants and shop owners and robbing underground gambling dens. Inevitably, some of the activities targeted were controlled by tong members. In response, many tongs started to hire rival gang members as protection. These alliances between tongs and some youth gangs further solidified the position of these gangs in the Chinatown communities.

As the 1970s progressed, Chinatown youth street gangs became inseparable from many tongs. Gangsters often lived in apartments rented for them by tongs and ate in restaurants owned by tong members. Despite being offered both jobs and membership by tongs, many gangs were often too volatile to be kept fully in check. As a result, Chinatown continued to experience violence and extortion at the hands of these youth gangs. Violent power struggles started to emerge as a result of gang turf wars and internal power shifts. The most powerful gangs carved up their territories, while the losers either collapsed or fled Chinatown.

In the 1970s, battles between Chinese gangs erupted in several US cities and for the first time in the twentieth century, the issue of Asian gang violence became widely featured in the media.

The Golden Dragon Massacre

A full-scale gang war broke out in San Francisco's Chinatown on Chinese New Year in 1972. The conflict started when gangster Joe Fong left the powerful Wah Ching gang and created his own gang, a group that consisted of both American and foreign-born Chinese. Fong called the new gang Chung Ching Yee. However, they became infamous under their street name: the Joe Boys.

The Wah Ching were furious at this betrayal and the competition it brought and vowed revenge. Soon after, the gangster rebel Fong (then only 19 years of age), found himself serving a life sentence in a California state prison on a murder charge. However, the Joe Boys continued without Fong and the conflict with the Wah Ching intensified with vicious battles over control of the illegal firecracker trade and protection rackets. Over the course of the next five years, fifty gangsters were killed in a series of confrontations that raged throughout the city of San Francisco.

By the summer of 1977, the conflict was still in full flow and with no end in sight. Things became even more violent when, at around two o'clock in the afternoon on the day after Memorial Day, 1977, 20-year old Kin Chuen Louie left his apartment in the Telegraph Hill area of the city. Louie was a former leader of the Hop Sing Boys (a Wah Ching ally) and he had been shot in the shoulder during a gang fight in September 1975. Louie was now a member of the Hop Sing Tong, a fraternal organization in Chinatown believed to have connections to criminal street gangs (a charge the tong denied). As Louie left his apartment that day, a gun wielding teenager ran at him. Seeing the gunman, Louie fled towards his car which was parked near Green Street. As he attempted to flee, he reversed his car into the vehicle parked behind him, slamming it into a telephone pole. Before Louie could drive away, the gunman opened fire. Twelve shots were fired from a .380 caliber Walther pistol, killing Louie instantly. San Francisco police never found the weapon or the killer.

On July 4th, violence once again flared up when a Wah Ching thug came into the Ping Yuen projects located on Pacific Avenue to collect money for firecracker sales. Waiting for him were members of the Joe Boys. As explained by ex Joe Boys gangster Bill Lee in his memoir, Chinese Playground: "It was Dodge City in Chinatown. Weapons were drawn and gunfire erupted, with gangsters running up and down the street, ducking behind cars and into doorways, blasting one another."

Violence had become so commonplace to Chinatown residents that the sound of gunshots became as ordinary as firecrackers on Independence Day. Casualties continued to pile up on that July 4th. Seventeen-year-old Joe Boys gangster Felix "Tiger" Huie was shot in the back and killed in the Ping Yuen projects. Another two Joe Boys gangsters and a Hop Sing Boy were wounded by gunfire. After Huie was killed, the situation escalated. Rival gangsters desecrated his grave with graffiti and urine, infuriating the Joe Boys. "It was now open season and 'no-holds barred'—no rules, no honor, no mercy. At stake was the control of Chinatown; independents against the Chinese underworld, and there were scores to settle."[5] The five-year feud had finally come to a head, and the Labor Day holiday was just around the corner.

The leader of the Joe Boys, Tom Yu, vowed revenge against the Wah Ching for the death of Huie. On September 3, 1977, Yu gathered the gang at his residence in Pacifica, a town in the southern suburbs of San Francisco. Although Yu was over eighteen, most of his underlings were younger. This use of young gang members was intentional. Yu knew that if his soldiers were arrested, they would only do limited time in juvenile detention since they were minors. Many of the battles in the San Francisco Chinatown gang wars were waged by these child soldiers.

The teenage Joe Boys fueled their anger with alcohol and weed, grabbed their weapons and waited. At 2 a.m., a call came to Yu. The Wah Ching chief Michael "Hot Dog" Louie and Frankie Lee of the Hop Sing Boys had been spotted in the Golden Dragon Restaurant on Washington Street in the Chinatown area of the city. Yu ordered the Joe Boys to attack.

The teen gangsters would wield serious firepower in the battle: "Melvin Yu (no relation to Tom Yu) prepared to do the most damage by taking a .45 caliber automatic assault rifle. Curtis Tam grabbed a sawed-off shotgun and Peter Ng carried a standard shotgun and a .38 handgun." The gangsters used a stolen Dodge Dart with Tom Yu's brother, Chester, doing the driving.

The Golden Dragon restaurant was a popular dining destination, especially during the late-night period as the restaurant was open until 3 a.m. It was also a popular destination for tourists as well as a venue for wedding receptions and dinners due to its large upstairs hall. Even at 2:40 a.m., when the Joe Boys hit-squad arrived, the restaurant was filled with 75 people in the main and upstairs dining areas.

---

[5] Calhoun, Bob. *Yesterday's Crimes: The War for Chinatown*. SF Weekly, 1 Sept. 2017.

Chester Yu parked the stolen car outside the restaurant and left it running. The gunmen slipped stockings over their heads and exited the car. Storming into the restaurant, they intended to kill as many rival gangsters as they could. One of Hot Dog's men saw the Joe Boys enter the restaurant and shouted, "Man with a gun!" This warning caused the Hop Sing Boys gangsters to dive onto the floor, which saved them. However, many of the civilian diners didn't understand what was happening and remained sitting upright, becoming easy targets.

Martin Yu opened fire first with his assault rifle. A hail of bullets splattered the main dining area. Tam and Ng followed by firing their shotguns into the mezzanine level (Tam would later claim he didn't kill anyone, instead stating that he fired his gun into an empty booth, confused. Feigning ignorance, Tam said, "I don't know my way around there. They don't have BART or a bus").

The shooting lasted only for around a minute, but it caused carnage. The gunmen fled, having killed five people and wounding another eleven. Not a single casualty had been a rival gangster. Until that time, this was the single worst mass shooting in San Francisco's long history. Many innocent civilians tragically lost their lives, including 48-year-old waiter Wong Fong, a father of seven children. A bullet severed his spine. "The other murder victims were Paul Wada, a law student at USF known for volunteer work; Denise Louie, who was visiting from Seattle; Calvin Fong, a Riordan High honor student; and Donald Kwan, a steel worker from West Portal. Surprisingly, there were two off-duty cops in the Golden Dragon when the gunfire erupted. Neither of them was able to get off a shot during the shooting; there were just too many people there."[6]

The shooting brought business in Chinatown to a sudden and dramatic halt. Deeply concerned, San Francisco Mayor George Moscone offered a $25,000 (soon increased to $100,000) reward for any information that could lead to convictions of the shooters involved in the Golden Dragon shooting. In March 1978, an informant came forward with information that led to the arrest of the gunmen. All the underage shooters were tried as adults and Tom Yu tried to cut a deal with the San Francisco prosecutor's office. However, this was rejected when it was revealed that Yu was the architect behind the mass shooting. Yu was later convicted of "five counts of murder, 11 counts of assault, and two counts of conspiracy." He was found guilty on all counts and received a life sentence.

The shooting led to the breakup of the Joe Boys after its members were convicted for their part in the massacre. Without their main rivals, the Wah Ching reigned supreme in Chinatown, but the landscape of law enforcement had changed permanently. Formerly ignored by the police while they targeted other gangsters, the high-profile Golden Dragon massacre forced the San Francisco Police department to establish an Asian Gang Task Force specifically to tackle Chinese gangs.

---

[6] Calhoun, Bob. *Yesterday's Crimes: The War for Chinatown*. SF Weekly, 1 Sept. 2017.

The Golden Dragon restaurant reopened after the shootings. However, in January 2006, it was closed due to health violations and later reopened as the Imperial Palace. It is currently still open, with "Golden Dragon Dining" in gold lettering on the storefront.

New Gangs Emerge

By the 1980s, Asian gangs had become larger and more sophisticated, aligning along ethnicity, space, and activity. Ethnicity for gangs was broken down between the Toisanese (also known as Taishanese) and Cantonese along with other ethnic youths like the Vietnamese, Fujianese, Hakka, and the Taiwanese. Chinatown gangs also spread beyond the boundaries of Chinatowns and even back to Asia. Because of this connection to organized crime in Asia, Chinatown gangs started to engage in more sophisticated criminal activities, such as heroin trafficking, human smuggling, money laundering, and credit card fraud.

The very existence of Chinese youth gangs remained relatively unknown in mainstream America until the notorious Golden Dragon massacre. Other sensational Chinese gang shootings followed and were widely covered in the media, raising the profile of Asian gangsters. In New York City on Christmas Eve, 1982, three gunmen shot indiscriminately into a bar, killing three people and wounding several others. On February 19, 1983, three thugs robbed the Wah Mee Club gambling house in Seattle's Chinatown. In a horrific act of violence, they tied up all 14 victims in the gambling house and shot them in the head one by one. Only one man survived the attack and was the key witness in a series of high-profile trials about the mass shooting.

Chinese youth gang warfare broke out in the cities of Los Angeles, Houston, Boston, Chicago, Vancouver, and Toronto. For many Americans, Chinatowns had become dangerous dens for gang violence, ruled by exotic and alien gangs. This cultural zeitgeist was exemplified by the release of Hollywood movies about Chinatown crime like China Girl (1975) and The Year of the Dragon (1985).

Faced with increasing violence and a series of high-profile shootings among Chinatown gangs, American law enforcement began to establish anti-Chinese gang taskforces throughout the various cities that were hardest hit by violent crime. The San Francisco Police Department, in response to the Golden Dragon massacre, set up the country's first Chinese gang taskforce. In 1977, the New York Police Department formed the Special Task Force.

American law enforcement, with a minority of Chinese or Asian officers, often had to learn about the cultural intricacies of policing Chinatown through first-hand exposure. In former NYPD officer John Timoney's memoir recounting his experiences patrolling Chinatown, he recalls: "During my time in Chinatown, I learned a lot about Chinese culture: the understanding of numbers and gambling and the roles that luck and the color red play in their world; the realization that the biggest gambling day in Chinatown was Monday, when the businesses were closed; the importance of male children within the family; and the importance of family itself. Shuck Seid would regularly provide me with Chinese proverbs neatly typed on small pink or red pads. One saying had to do with worrying about the snow in front of your own door and not concerning yourself with the snow on another man's roof. Loosely translated, it referred to an individual's loyalty and where that loyalty should be concentrated. In some respects, this is counter to many of our Western notions. For example, the great hero in Western culture is the Good Samaritan, someone who is willing to endanger his own life to help others. This notion permeates our literature and, in modern times, our movies—Gary Cooper, in the movie High Noon, epitomizes the Good Samaritan. Chinese culture does not view the Good Samaritan as favorably. Their rationale is that a man's first obligation is to his family, and that the Good Samaritan, by getting involved in other people's business, risks his own existence and therefore that of his family unit and his role within it."

During the 1980s, several new street gangs such as Fuk China, White Tigers, Tung On, Green Dragons, Golden Star, and Born To Kill all emerged in New York Chinatown, Queens and Brooklyn. This surge in gang activity was the result of a new wave of Chinese immigration and the establishment of many new Chinese-owned and operated businesses as well as the high-profile nature of Chinese gangsters, a factor that attracted many new gang members keen to share the notoriety.

Chinese gangs also spread to cities outside the major urban Chinatowns in places such as Oakland, Houston, Falls Church, Arlington, Philadelphia, Chicago, and Boston. American law enforcement started to classify Chinese street gangs as organized crime and by the 1990s, all major Asian street gangs had been indicted as racketeering enterprises.

The FBI Reacts

Despite the increased law enforcement attention in Chinatowns, the list of sensational Chinese related gang crimes continued to grow. In 1982, a white female tourist was raped and murdered by several Chinese gangsters in New York's Chinatown. In 1984, a Chinese American writer was shot in Daly City, California. This murder was orchestrated by the Taiwan-based United Bamboo Triad. For the first time, Chinese gang-related activity in America had started to involve people outside the Chinese residents of Chinatown. As mainstream America started to see the effects of Chinese crime in the media, the public began to demand law enforcement act to provide increased protection from these increasingly powerful crime groups.

In response to the murder of the white female tourist, the NYPD, FBI, and the Manhattan District Attorney's Office conducted a two-year investigation into the criminal gangs responsible for the murder. Their main focus was on the Ghost Shadows, a powerful street gang based in New York's Chinatown. The Ghost Shadows gang was formed in the early 1970s by migrants from Taiwan and Hong Kong and was claimed to have an affiliation with the On Leon Tong.

A total of 90 detectives and FBI agents were assigned to the joint taskforce to investigate the Ghost Shadows. They also managed to recruit several former members of the gang as informants. The taskforce was extremely successful and a total of 25 leaders and members of the Ghost Shadows were eventually indicted under the RICO Act (Racketeer Influenced and Corrupt Organizations Act). This was the first time a Chinese gang in America had been indicted by law enforcement under federal racketeering charges. However, despite this success by law enforcement, the Ghost Shadows continue to be a factor in the New York gang scene.

The 1994 murder of Chinese-American writer Henry Liu in Daly City, a short distance south of San Francisco was investigated by both the NYPD and FBI. Liu was a US citizen who originally came from Taiwan and had attracted the interest of the government in that country with a series of critical articles in the US press. The investigation seemed to prove that Taiwanese officials had conspired with members of the Taiwan-based United Bamboo Triad. During the investigation, two undercover FBI agents even managed to have themselves formally inducted into the organization. As a direct result of this investigation, nine high-ranking gang members were arrested in New York, Los Angeles, Houston, and Las Vegas, and all were charged with violations under the RICO Act. Tung Kuei-sen, an alleged hit-man working for United Bamboo was charged with the murder of Liu.

Law enforcement pressure continued to increase in the 1980s due to a major criminal component of Chinese gangs—heroin. In the 1990s, there were more Chinese street gangs in New York City than in any other American city, making New York the epicenter of Chinese organized crime in America. Many of these gangs were becoming heavily involved in the international heroin trade. Although the majority of heroin imported illegally into the US comes from Mexico, by the late 1980s, Chinese traffickers had become sufficiently important players in the heroin trade that the Drug Administration Agency (DEA) in New York City set up the Asian Heroin Group, part of the Organized Crime Drug Enforcement Strike Force, designed to deal specifically with Asian drug smuggling.

This taskforce was known as Group Z-41 and was able to shut down several prominent Asian smuggling rings. Since many of these Chinese traffickers were either in America on temporary visas or illegally, law enforcement also sought assistance from the Immigration and Naturalization Service (INS) to deal with Chinese crime groups. The INS was responsible for screening Chinese visa applicants and deporting those with serious crime convictions. This INS connection would be of great importance as many of the Chinese criminals convicted were involved in transnational crime, such as heroin trafficking and human smuggling.

Violence continued to be commonplace among the Chinese gangs in America during the early 1990s. The murders of federal witnesses by the ruthless Born-to-Kill and Green Dragons gangs accelerated the NYPD and FBI efforts to stop these two gangs from further carnage. The Green Dragons became particularly notorious in New York City. Based in the suburb of Elmhurst (which has a large Asian population), this gang comprising young men of Chinese origin, soon challenged established Chinese street gangs such as the White Tigers. This culminated in a planned shootout between members of the Green Dragons and White Tigers in Elmhurst in November 1990. However, the NYPD and FBI investigation became aware of the intended battle and, instead of members of the White Tigers, the Green Dragons instead found themselves facing-off against heavily armed police. Sixteen members of the gang were arrested and charged with offences including racketeering and murder.

Born To Kill (BTK) was a Vietnamese gang based in New York's Manhattan Chinatown. By 1990 this gang was believed to have more than eighty members and was involved in prostitution, the production of counterfeit goods and the widespread extortion of small businesses. Initially this gang was believed to have had affiliation with Triad groups and existing Chinese organized crime groups such as the Flying Dragons. However, it gradually dissociated itself from groups of Chinese ethnicity and became one of the largest and most feared gangs within the Vietnamese/American community in the New York area and in other areas including Texas and Mississippi. In 1991 the gang's leader, David Thai, was arrested with a number of other senior members of the gang at a safe house on Long Island following a long FBI/NYPD investigation.

Stopping human smuggling also became a central mission for federal agencies. All this increased federal attention resulted in seven major Chinese gangs in New York, San Francisco, and Boston being indicted on RICO charges between 1990 and 1994. By the end of 1994, only the Wah Ching in San Francisco had escaped federal racketeering charges. All the other major Chinese gangs in America had been significantly damaged by federal and police investigations.

The Connection Between Youth Gangs and Tongs

For most outsiders, the connection between triads, tongs and youth gangs is not easily discerned. All are believed to be involved in crime to some extent, but all appear to be quite separate groups with their own membership and agendas. However, one of the outcomes of the ongoing investigations in the early 1990s, including the induction of several FBI agents as members of various Chinese organized crime groups, was a much better understanding of the relationships between these groups.

A distinctive element of Chinatown gangs is the often-intimate connection between the mainly youth street gangs like the Wah Ching and Ghost Shadows and adult tong groups. As noted by author Ko-lin Chin in his book Chinatown Gangs: "The emergence of a new, powerful adult organization is the prerequisite to the formation of the youth gangs in the community. The expansion of existing adult organizations or the appearance of new ones produces social tensions and instability in the relative positions of the existing organizations, compelling some groups to seek monopoly control over important territories and resources."[7]

Conflicts between adult groups attempting to defend their territories often led to the recruitment of members of local youth gangs. This in turn led to long-term connections between adult groups and youth gangs which are "seen as a strategic use of resources to avoid interorganizational dependencies among adult groups that are striving for autonomy and independence."[8]

Adult associations are able to achieve great influence in the community as new migrants arrive, increasing their ranks and membership. The more members a tong organization is able to recruit into the fold, the more power it wields. For instance, the Fukien American Association is a prime example of this process in action. Although it was established in the late 1940s, the association did not reach its apex until waves of Chinese immigrants started to arrive in great numbers from the Fujian province in Southern China in the 1970s and 1980s. As donations increased from wealthier members, the association was able to purchase a huge building in Manhattan's Chinatown, which was used as a headquarters. An impressive association building was imperative to its success. It showed that the association was able and willing to help its members and powerful enough to ensure their loyalty.

The Fukien American Association is a legal association ostensibly dedicated to providing help and guidance for Chinese migrants in America. However, an FBI investigation in the 1990s revealed that this association had close links with Fuk Ching gang, based in New York City. The Fuk Ching are one of the most powerful, and transnationally active Chinese organized crime

---

[7] Chin, Ko-lin. *Chinatown Gangs: Extortion, Enterprise, and Ethnicity*. Oxford University Press, 2000.
[8] Ibid.

groups and members used the Fukien American Association building in Manhattan as their headquarters.

The precise nature of the relationship between the Fukien American Association and the Fuk Ching gang is still a matter for debate, but it seems that the tong association allowed the Fuk Ching to operate on their territory, thus legitimizing the gang in the eyes of many members of the Chinese migrant community, and may have used gang members to protect illegal tong activities such as gambling operations and may even have supplied the gang with money and weapons. The precise nature of the relationship between these groups is very difficult for law enforcement to accurately define, in part because of the way in which communication between the groups are carried out.

Within the tong a person is usually nominated as ah kung (grandfather) or shuk foo (uncle) for a particular gang. That person within the tong has sole responsibility for communication with the gang. Within the gang, one member is designated as dai dai lo (big big brother). All communications between the groups are handled between face-to-face meetings between the shuk foo and dai dai lo, leaving no written or telephonic trail for investigators to follow.

However, the development of a new Chinese migrant adult organization or association did not always lead to the creation of a youth street gang. Some of these organizations were concerned solely with maintaining legitimate elements of social order. Sometimes, different organizations found themselves in conflict with other groups, legitimate or illegal, and in many cases these disputes were resolved through the American court system rather than by employing young thugs to fight on their behalf. This distinction led to conflicts between tongs associated with organized crime and those who stayed within the law.

This is illustrated by the story of the Chinese-American Planning Council (CPC), a multi-functional social service agency based in New York City. As it evolved over the years into a powerful community organization, the CPC became influential enough to challenge the existing order of Manhattan Chinatown, and this infuriated many of the traditional associations. This bitter conflict between the CPC and the tongs reached a crescendo when the CPC tried to exclude tong members from the board of a residential project in New York City. The CPC accused the tong of organized crime activities and the tongs lost the power struggle and withdrew their candidates in defeat.

However, the distinction between organizations that sought legitimate avenues and those who pursued illegitimate power was not always clear-cut and sometimes, either could lead to the formation of a youth gang. Sometimes, even groups pursuing illegal activities such as gambling made a decision to avoid involvement with criminal gangs. However, most groups involved in illegal activities would assure their safety by forming an alliance with an existing gang and in this way, they avoided violent conflict with other existing gangs. The Tsung Tsin Association, a social and cultural association for Chinese migrants, is a good example of this. As they involved themselves in gambling operations, they allied with the Tung On Association, a tong group which was located on the same street. They hired Tung On gangsters for protection, thus avoiding any possibility of violent conflict.

Any new organization being established within an American Chinatown has to take elaborate precautions in order to not challenge the authority of a complex web of interconnected existing legal and illegal organizations within the same area. These include: "a claim to a certain area (normally the street where its headquarters are located) as its territory; a disclosure of political orientations; a request to business owners within its territory to join it; and the establishment of its own gambling places."[9]

When a new organization claims territory or attempts to enter the lucrative gambling industry, other existing organizations often react strongly and even violently. This is particularly true when the new organization's territory overlaps with another's turf, thus offering direct competition.

In 1982, a former Hip Sing member established a new association, the Kam Lun Association. He chose a headquarters location on East Broadway in Manhattan's Chinatown. He also owned a gambling establishment at the same location. Problems started when he claimed East Broadway as Kam Lun territory and solicited local businessmen in the area to join his new association. He even hired gangsters from the Flying Dragons, a youth gang aligned with the Hip Sing, to guard his gambling den and territory. It seemed inevitable that the Kam Lun would become a powerful player in Chinatown. But in December 1982, all of it came to a halt when three Hip Sing gunmen burst into an East Broadway bar and opened fire. They were targeting Kum Lun members. Three were killed and another eight were grievously wounded. The mass shooting, dubbed the Golden Star Massacre, was the catalyst that crushed the Kam Lun. Shortly after, the association virtually disappeared from Chinatown.

Because of these conflicts between the adult organizations, the youth members of the organizations were able to integrate as cohesive units. The leaders of these adult organizations in turn provided these youths a place to congregate (most likely a room in their headquarters, close to the gambling den). While the adult leaders in the organization might not always intend to form a youth gang within their association, the constant presence of younger people at the headquarters was usually welcomed as it provided a ready source of troops to strengthen the group's territorial claims and increase protection.

There are two main factors to consider when trying to understand the social transformation of Chinatown youth groups into gangs. Professor Joan Moore, an expert on the social structure of gangs, stated in her 1978 study that "negative societal reaction is a crucial factor in the process of gang formation." In terms of Chinatowns, the large numbers of young people hanging out at the

---

[9] Chin, Ko-lin. *Chinatown Gangs: Extortion, Enterprise, and Ethnicity.* Oxford University Press, 2000.

association headquarters or outside its gambling dens might attract unwanted attention from law enforcement. When these young people were arrested, law enforcement would often label them as members of a street gang. For example, a group of youths with connections to the Tung On Association became known by police as the Tung On gang, and the Fujianese youth at the Fukien American Association became labeled as the Fuk Ching (Fujianese youth) gang. Eventually, the names used by the police became adopted by the young people themselves and the identification of gang names became a self-fulfilling prophecy that actually led in some cases to the creation of these gangs.

Another factor is the dynamics of societal reaction, which means that the "ability of the affiliated adult organization to successfully sustain itself and remain in existence is also important in the formation of a youth gang and in its ability to thrive."[10] For the Kam Lun Association, for example, it was unable to survive after the Golden Star Massacre, forcing the aligned youth group to be dissolved. These youth groups can then be transformed into more permanent gangs, but only if the sponsoring adult organization is "capable of growing and maintaining themselves amidst adversity."[11] New youth groups are especially vulnerable to more established youth gangs and the adult associations.

As adult organizations expand in influence, the associated youth groups also grow in power. With the support of adult organizations, gangsters extort money from local business owners in their territory, collect money and protect gambling establishments. All these activities help legitimize their existence in the community.

Both adult organizations and youth gangs depend on each other for resources and capabilities. Alone, adult organizations may be incapable of mustering the manpower resources needed to achieve their goals and "this necessitates a cluster of transactions that effect exchanges with street gangs and inevitably link the two types of organizations."[12] The specific relationship between individual youth gangs and adult organizations also depends on shared mutual interests and can vary greatly based on their complexity, intensity, and prominence.

These gang activities have been active in the American Chinese community for decades and most experts seem to agree that they are unlikely to disappear in the foreseeable future. A combination of factors contribute to this state of affairs: "The isolation of the Chinese community, the inability of American law enforcement authorities to penetrate the Chinese criminal underworld, and the reluctance of Chinese victims to come forward for help all conspire to enable Chinese gangs to endure."[13]

---

[10] Chin, Ko-lin. University *Chinatown Gangs: Extortion, Enterprise,* and Ethnicity. Oxford Press, 2000.
[11] Ibid.
[12] Ibid.
[13] Ibid.

Adult organizations provided valuable services in the Chinese communities. However, some of these services are illegal and may include gambling and prostitution. The youth gangs are employed by the organizations to protect these business ventures from the police and other gangs. The gangsters provide both order and customer safety. Due to the adult organizations lack of sufficient muscle to enforce their territories, young gangsters also maintain the integrity of adult criminal territories as street soldiers. Business owners within the boundaries of the organization are often intimidated by the gangsters, causing them to donate or join the adult organizations to avoid being shaken down by the gangs.

Individual adult members also occasionally use gangs to solidify their own positions of power within the organization and the community. Internal power struggles are common within organizations and a good relationship with street gangs by high ranking organization members ensures a steady supply of muscle should a power struggle turn violent. Gangs can also be used by association leaders to improve their standing in the community. Anyone who wants to do business within the community must obtain the leader's opinion by offering either money or partnerships.

The Life and Times of Kwok Cheung Chow, aka Shrimp Boy

The way in which gang membership can provide a route to power and influence can be illustrated by the example of the life and career of one of the most notorious Chinese gangsters in America, a man who became known as Shrimp Boy. A lifelong street gangster, Shrimp Boy was involved in some of the most famous criminal cases in Chinatown, including the Golden Dragon shooting (he survived by diving onto the floor). His life is typical of many of the immigrant gangsters of Chinatown during this era.

Kwok Cheung Chow was born in Hong Kong in 1959 and he received his nickname from his grandmother because he was so small. Hailing from a middle-class background, Shrimp Boy's father owned a barbershop; however, fortunes turned when he was eight years old. His father lost the barbershop due to a series of gambling debts, forcing Shrimp Boy, his three brothers, grandmother, and parents to move from their nice apartment to a tiny one-room apartment with no running water.

A mere year later, the rundown building where Shrimp Boy's family lived had burned down, forcing the family to move again. In this new home, there were only two beds. Every night, Shrimp Boy tried to sleep next to his grandmother, who he clung onto for comfort. With these tough early childhood experiences, Shrimp Boy was already a hardened kid by the age of nine. He fought often, earning a reputation for bravado and scrappy willpower. Shrimp Boy was small in stature and often told people around him tall tales of winning fights he had actually lost. This bravado caught the attention of a local street gangster, who took the young Shrimp Boy under his wing, teaching him "the ancient Chinese gang code of loyalty, trust, honor, dignity, and respect, as well as the value of keeping a knife tucked in the waistband of your pants."[14]

In a short time, Shrimp Boy was working for his gangster mentor, running a series of street errands, such as being a courier for small bags of heroin. Before long, Shrimp Boy would accompany his mentor to fights. During one brawl, his mentor was being beaten and was losing the fight. Seeing the situation deteriorate, Shrimp Boy jumped into the fray, pulling out a huge watermelon knife. With two swift strokes, Shrimp Boy cracked the heavy blade on the opponent's head, exposing bone. This fight made Shrimp Boy a local gangster legend and he relished the fame.

In 1976, Shrimp Boy was 17 and his family made a major decision: they would leave Hong Kong and move to San Francisco. According to Shrimp Boy, he was already a hardened street thug at this point, with time spent in juvenile detention and a code of never talking to the police, no matter what the circumstances. Arriving in America, Shrimp Boy carried an unusual document—a letter of recommendation from his Hong Kong gang leader—which he gave to an elder in Chinatown. Forgoing school, the seasoned street gangster sought to climb the local Chinatown tong ranks.

Shrimp Boy quickly gained a reputation for extreme violence. When he was 17, he was sent by a Hop Sing Tong lieutenant to a house in suburban Hillsborough, New Jersey. The mission was a violent one. The tongs had been hired by the Italian mafia to pay a visit to the resident of the house. Shrimp Boy arrived at the house, dressed casually in "bell bottoms, a jeans jacket and platform shoes." He took a two-by-four that was near the front door, rang the doorbell and proceeded to beat senseless the man who answered, causing injuries serious enough to warrant a three-month hospital stay. The whole incident took two minutes. The next day, after the brutal attack, a tong boss met Shrimp Boy at a Chinatown restaurant and slid him an envelope containing $3,000 cash.

Like all street gangsters, Shrimp Boy regarded being arrested as simply an occupational hazard. Shrimp Boy's first arrest and conviction came in 1978 when he was charged with armed robbery. He had robbed a gambling den. Sentenced to 11 years at San Quentin, Shrimp Boy was not deterred from violence simply because he was in prison. While there, he beat a man senseless with a food tray, describing the action as being similar to swinging a tennis racket: ''backhand, forehand, backhand, forehand.'' The incident landed him in solitary confinement. While serving hard time, a prison psychologist recommended to Shrimp Boy that he should seek a profession unrelated to criminal activity. Shrimp Boy listened to the advice and attempted to become a deep-sea welder. However, his studies were interrupted when a prison riot broke out and the training facility was shut down. He dove back into the underworld by dealing heroin in prison.

In 1985, Shrimp Boy was released from San Quentin and he took a bus to San Francisco and tried to look for a normal job. But that proved to be a short-lived ambition as he eventually noticed several pretty girls outside a Vietnamese noodle shop. After talking with them, he

---

[14] Weil, Elizabeth. *SHRIMP BOY'S DAY IN COURT*. New York Times Magazine, Oct 18, 2015, pp. 36-41, 59, 12.

realized they were prostitutes and Shrimp Boy saw an opportunity to make money in the sex trade. He convinced some of the girls to leave and work for him. Within a few months, Shrimp Boy had rented a big Victorian house and proceeded to run a successful brothel. Business was so lucrative that according to Shrimp Boy, he was making more money than he knew what to do with. He tried to solve this by pushing his cash profits into several enterprises: "cocaine distribution, fencing stolen weapons, Rolexes, jewelry and pills."

But according to Shrimp Boy, he wanted to live a normal life, free of crime. In 1989, in an attempt to make his mother proud, Shrimp Boy tried once again to go clean. His mother even gave a "ritual bath with grapefruit leaves, to cleanse his spirit." Shrimp Boy eventually found work at the Lucky Market in Daly City, bagging groceries for $4.50 an hour. He worked hard and was soon promoted to janitorial staff, making $7.25. However, a member of the San Francisco Police Department's gang taskforce called the supermarket boss, who became suspicious and Shrimp Boy was forced to leave his job.

Although his next employment as a bodyguard was legitimate, he found himself on a slippery slope back into criminal life. One night while working a security position at a casino in Oakland, Shrimp Boy, dressed professionally, caught the eye of Peter Chong, a leader in the Hong Kong Triad known as Wo Hop To. Peter was on an ambitious mission in the United States—he was attempting to unite the East and West Coast heroin trades under a single banner. Before Shrimp Boy knew it, he was discussing these plans with Peter in Golden Gate Park. Shrimp Boy was back in the gangster game.

In April 1992, Shrimp Boy flew to New York on a business trip to discuss mergers with gang leaders in Chinatown. He was arrested there on 48 counts, including "RICO activities (the acronym refers to charges under the Racketeer Influenced and Corrupt Organizations Act), conspiracy to distribute heroin and cocaine, murder for hire, cocaine possession, arson, unlicensed firearm sales and transfers and a slew of interstate commerce crimes—so many charges that the government split the case into two trials."[15] Peter Chong, sensing an imminent law enforcement crackdown, fled back to Hong Kong.

Shrimp Boy was an old-school gangster, one who lived by the code of never talking to the police. Gangsters never snitched. However, to his disgust, during his trial many of his former associates were brought to the stand and testified against him. He was found guilty on six counts and sentenced to 24 years. Peter Chong was eventually extradited to America, where the triad leader also betrayed Shrimp Boy. According to Shrimp Boy, his world collapsed: "a gangster without a code or crew is just a lone felon."

In 2000, he accepted a plea deal and ratted out his former associates. "Documents show that the government promised him a new life under the witness-protection program, an S visa

---

[15] Ibid.

(residence for a witness who assists law enforcement) and release on time served. In exchange, Shrimp Boy would testify against Chong. (Chong served time for racketeering and was released in 2008.) Shrimp Boy describes this act of testifying—aiding the United States attorney, selling out his onetime partner and the only set of values he had ever known—as the hardest experience of his life."[16]

Because of the assistance he had given police investigators and the District Attorney's Office, Shrimp Boy was released from prison in 2003. However, he soon drifted back into criminal activity, becoming head of a criminal faction within the Ghee Kung Tong.

In 2014, Chow was arrested during an FBI raid concerned with racketeering and corruption. His trial began in 2015 and in 2016 he was found guilty on all one hundred and sixty-two charges. He was sentenced to two life terms, one for racketeering and one for the 2006 murder of prominent Chinatown leader Allen Leung as well as being given an additional twenty-year sentence for other charges. During the trial, the prosecution likened Chow to a Mafia Godfather and called him the "sun of the underworld universe." It seems unlikely that Shrimp Boy will ever leave Federal prison.

Suburban Gangsters

The popular conception of gangs, especially youth gangs, associates them with run-down, urban areas of US cities. However, in terms of Asian gangs, a recent phenomenon has involved the growth of gangs in relatively affluent suburbs leading to something entirely new: the middle-class gangster. This is most notable in some cities in California.

A study of Taiwanese gangsters in suburban Southern California in 2008 (conducted by scholars from California State University, Northridge, Florida International University, University of Kansas, and the National Institute on Drug Abuse) revealed several interesting facts about the changing nature of Chinese gangs in America. For example, the study revealed that these Taiwanese gangs did not have gang tattoos, gang signs, or specific clothing or colors associated with their respective gangs. The study looked not just at Asian but also Latino gangs and an interesting fact was noted. Part of the study allowed researchers to offer their gangster interview subjects compensation of $50 to participate in the study. All the Latino gangsters accepted the money. However, none of the Taiwanese gangsters took the money as they considered the amount to be too small to be worth their time, an indicator of the unique nature of these middle-class suburban street gangs.

Like all street gangs, the Taiwanese gangsters in Southern California participated in many classic criminal activities. These included "gang fights, street-level drug sales, drug use, home invasion, extortion, robbery, burglary, credit card frauds, and the receiving and selling of stolen

---

[16] Ibid.

property."[17] A large part of their social life also revolved around their respective gangs, with members spending much of their personal time with their fellow gangsters.

However, a key difference between these suburban Taiwanese gangsters and other urban street gangs (like their Latino counterparts in California) was socioeconomic class. In comparison to the Latinos, the Southern California Taiwanese gangsters were relatively affluent in terms of both economic and cultural capital. They came from middle to upper middle-class families with parents in professional or entrepreneurial backgrounds. Most of the Taiwanese gangsters interviewed for the study came from the cities of Diamond Bar, Rowland Heights, and Hacienda Heights in Los Angeles County. In the year 2000, all these cities had a median household income of $60,000, greatly exceeding the cities in the study that focused on Latino gangs. Because of these socioeconomic privileges, the Taiwanese gangsters were able to use significant cultural, economic, and social capital to access both higher and professional education. This privilege gave them an opportunity to pursue a future outside the criminal underclass and gave them a route back into a professional career and normal society.

In the study, every Taiwanese gang member that was interviewed gave their family status as middle-class or above. In fact, only two subjects even reported family money problems. This was also very different compared to the Chinese gangsters interviewed in previous studies (most studies on Asian gangsters focused on Chinatowns, generally a working class, urban environment). The subjects in the 2008 study generally described their parents as either professionals or entrepreneurs with careers in Taiwan or America. Some subjects even reported that their parents were high-ranking Taiwanese government officials, businessmen or held other prestigious roles.

Because of their highly educated parents, many Taiwanese gangsters faced pressure from their families to pursue college and white-collar careers. In fact, their parents often made significant efforts to ensure that outcome. This focus on professional careers can be seen by the fact that several subjects in the study had already completed a bachelor's degree while others were enrolled in various colleges, with one subject even possessing an advanced degree from a prestigious Southern California university.

Most of those who were not in higher education still had high school diplomas or were enrolled in school with intentions of pursuing college in the future. Furthermore, all the subjects also claimed to be good students with impressive academic records, even going so far as telling the researchers that they were "good students at school with good grades and as having good relationships with teachers, counselors, and their schools."[18] The Taiwanese gangsters in the study all viewed higher education as a critically important part of their future.

---

[17] Pih, Kay Kei-Ho, et al. *Different Strokes for Different Gangs? An Analysis of Capital Among Latino and Asian Gang Members*. Sociological Perspectives, vol. 51, no. 3, 2008, pp. 473–494.
[18] Ibid.

This was notably different to most other street gangs, where most members lacked formal education and the socio-economic advantages that this conferred. This focus on education by the Taiwanese gangsters could be connected to several cultural factors. Unlike other American street gangs, typical Taiwanese gangsters were only involved in gang life for two to three years, a relatively short amount of time when compared to their non-Asian counterparts. Taiwanese gangsters often quit their gangs to avoid shaming their families and to avoid the possibility of jeopardizing their future professional careers.

Leaving the gang life for most Taiwanese gangsters frequently involved more than just family and personal feelings. In most cases, the ability to make money in a stable career were closely linked to the gangsters leaving criminal life behind. Most Taiwanese gangsters left their respective gangs in order to not hinder their potential in the legitimate economy, thus causing them to "move on."

Perhaps most interesting was the fact that Taiwanese gangsters often continued to attend school and maintain good grades, all while being involved in gang life. Staying in school was partly due to parental pressure, but the gangsters themselves were clearly aware of the connection between financial success and educational attainment. Therefore, participation in higher education at university was seen as critical to many Taiwanese gangsters even while they were fully engaged in their gang activities. Many gangsters also claimed they could make more money through legitimate methods with the aid of their families than through illicit means in the underworld. This seemingly contradictory double life makes these suburban Asian gangsters quite unique among street gangs in America. According to the 2008 study, these Taiwanese gangsters seemed very capable of juggling simultaneously being good students and low-level criminals.

Socioeconomic mobility was a key reason behind the ability for Taiwanese gangsters to disassociate from gang life. This could be accomplished by moving to another neighborhood or city to create distance from an existing social circle, something that was critical to leaving gang life. Many Taiwanese gangsters accomplished this by moving away for college or careers in other cities. Because of their access to financial resources from their families or their own legitimate careers, they possessed the resources and capability to physically distance themselves from their fellow gangsters should they wish to leave criminal life. The parents of these gang members often provided significant assistance to these individuals in the event they wished to move on to more legitimate pursuits.

The ability to relocate was very important, as most gangsters reported that it was extremely difficult to leave gang life without creating physical distance between them and their former friends. In almost all street gangs, quitting the group was punishable through violence, and at times, death. By virtue of moving away, the action gave transitioning gangsters a sense of safety as they separated themselves from the criminal life. This freedom to leave gang life through socioeconomic means made Southern Californian Taiwanese gangs unique when compared to their counterparts from other ethnic groupings. For example, economic mobility was generally much rarer for members of Latino gangs in California due to less access to family wealth and education.

If socioeconomic reasons were not the primary motivators for joining gang activity, then why did these young Taiwanese join gangs in Southern California? The key to understanding this is the concept of social capital. According to French academic Pierre Bourdieu, "networks of specific social relationships carry social capital to permit or even engender further reward-seeking actions to take place."[19] This is important because criminology scholars argue that gangs offer multiple forms of social capital. Gangs "operate primarily as additional networks of individuals providing resources and opportunities in illicit and licit economic actions."[20] For example, the friends and family members of gang members were often the initial drug sources for their criminal activities. For most street gangs—because of their limited access to legitimate sources of income due to living in economically deprived neighborhoods—they depended on illegal activities such as selling drugs for financial gain.

As a result, gang activity was heavily involved in interpersonal and economic networks. But these were also important for consolidating business and personal security in hazardous environments. Gangs were able to provide individuals with a range of resources that were unique to their immediate socioeconomic environments, including protection and security. While most gang members did not need to participate in the drug trade, these economic opportunities were possible due to the social capital created by their gang connections.

This concept was interesting when focused on Taiwanese gangs. Most Taiwanese gangsters had access to legitimate institutions, and cultural and economic capital. Therefore, gang enlistment served to satisfy "fascination, excitement and a supplementary form of social capital."[21] For Taiwanese gangsters, gang involvement was the result of friendships with gang members and access to the prestige that comes with power, status, and sex appeal. Money was not a huge factor for Taiwanese gang membership. Instead, the primary benefit was future gains made possible by their gang network connections, and not short-term monetary gains from illicit activities. Because of this focus on networking for the future, often into legitimate enterprises, the line between legal and illegal opportunities was often murky. Friendships formed in the gangs translated into business ventures in the legitimate economy, even after gang membership was over. As stated by one Taiwanese gangster in the research study in 2008, "My family is rich, I do not need money."[22]

Many Taiwanese gangsters also reported that their families offered them financial capital after they graduated from college. In addition to money, these family connections also extended to

---

[19] Ibid.
[20] Ibid.
[21] Ibid.
[22] Ibid.

"stock and real estate deals, merchandise supplies, and other business necessities."[23] Gang membership became a source of auxiliary social capital. This is illustrated by the example of one Taiwanese gangster in the 2008 study:

> "One Southern California respondent, upon graduating with an advanced degree from a major local university, worked as a financial consultant at a leading investment firm. The services he currently provides and his position in the investment firm are legitimate and legal. However, a sizeable portion of his current clientele was based on interpersonal relationships established when he was a gang lieutenant. Another respondent also admitted that acquaintances and connections made in gangs were extremely important for his future business investments. The same respondent is currently operating a chain of legitimate small businesses in the aforementioned Southern California cities. He disclosed that several of his business partners and investors were either former or current gang members or elders. He admitted these connections were made during his active involvement in gangs. Even though he claimed he was no longer involved with his former gang, certain useful contacts and networks were maintained for business purposes. Friends, associates, and connections in gangs and the illegitimate economy constitute a vast network of potential business opportunities, partners, and even venture capital. The successful pursuit of both legitimate and illegitimate economic interests of these respondents are heavily rooted in the interpersonal relationships generated through gangs, again suggesting that a substantial amount of social capital is located and embedded in the gangs."

The middle-class Taiwanese gangsters formed an interesting counterpoint to their Latino and African-American gang counterparts. For many of the Taiwanese gangsters, membership in a gang was seen as simply a step on the road to a legitimate life, a brief foray into crime before adopting the responsibilities of adulthood. This is in stark contrast to many other gang members who found themselves trapped in criminal life because they lacked the resources and education to do anything else.

As Chinese immigration continues in America, the unique cultural elements of Chinese gangs will continue to thrive in Chinatowns, even though the socioeconomic class and regional origins of Chinese immigrants have changed over the decades. The first Chinese immigrants hailed primarily from the southern Cantonese speaking areas of China. These were working-class people who opened laundromats, restaurants, and grocery stores. They relied on urban Chinatowns for their economic and social networks. However, the modern wave of Chinese immigrants has come mostly from Mandarin speaking areas in mainland China and Taiwan, and in the case of New York City, the Fujian province of Southern China. A key element is that many recent Chinese immigrants also tend to be more middle class, are educated, and are wealthier than previous generations who arrived in Chinatown more out of necessity than choice.

---

[23] Ibid.

This trend can clearly be seen in the development of new Chinese suburbs in Southern California, the Bay Area and Washington State. Crime has followed this immigration wave as well, demonstrated by the development of suburban Taiwanese youth gangs—street level criminals of a decidedly more middle class and affluent background. Compared to the more traditional Chinatown street gangs, these new Taiwanese street gangs are better educated, often coming from highly privileged families. As China continues to grow in both economic and international power, Chinese gangs in America will evolve and adapt to the new dynamics of both culture and socioeconomic class and it seems that Asian gangs and organised crime will remain a feature of US cities for the foreseeable future.

Free Books by Charles River Editors

We have brand new titles available for free most days of the week. To see which of our titles are currently free, click on this link.

Discounted Books by Charles River Editors

We have titles at a discount price of just 99 cents everyday. To see which of our titles are currently 99 cents, click on this link.